For

CHRISTMAS
A Time For Family

Compiled by Lois L. Kaufman

Illustrated by Barbara Chiantia
Designed by Lesley Ehlers

Peter Pauper Press, Inc.
White Plains, New York

Contents

The Christmas Miracle

On the morning before the Christmas that fell when I was six, my father took my brother and me for a walk in the woods of the Old Colony town where we lived. Three times as we walked he stopped, and cut a small balsam tree. There was a very tiny one, hardly more than a seedling; a small one a foot or so high; and a youthful one of perhaps four feet. So we each had a tree to bear, flaglike, back to the house. It didn't occur to us single-minded larvae that this had the least connection with Christmas. Our father was a botanist Ph.D., given to plucking all manner of specimens whenever we walked, with the offhand explanation, "A fine *Tsuga canadensis*," or whatever it was. By nightfall we had forgotten all about the walk.

For this was Christmas Eve, and we were suddenly in a panic. Where was The Tree? On experience, we knew that it was usually delivered in the morning, that Father set it up in the afternoon and that Mother trimmed it at night, letting us help with the ornaments before

she put us to bed in a fever of anticipation. But this year we had seen no tree arrive; look where we would, we could not find one; and even Mother turned aside our questions. Would there be no Tree? Would there, perhaps, be no Christmas at all for us? How we wished now, that we had not put the cat in the milk-pail!

But after supper Father and Mother took us into the sitting-room. In a cleared corner over by the big closet stood a jar of earth. "Christmas," said Father, "is a day of miracles, to remind us of the greatest Miracle of all. Perhaps we shall see one." Then Mother led us out, closing the door on Father and the jar of earth—and the closet.

"We can help," she said, "by learning this song." And she began, softly but very true, "O Little Town of Bethlehem." We tried hard in our shrill way. But even Mother had to admit it was only a good try. Yet when the door opened and we went again into the sitting-room, behold! A tiny Tree had appeared in the jar of earth! Hardly more than a seedling, to be sure, and not old enough yet to bear ornaments, but indubitably a Tree. Marveling, we went out again.

This time we did better—on the words, if not the tune. And when we re-entered the sitting-room, the Tree had grown—to perhaps a foot or

so in height! A blaze of hope flashed upon us. We went out and tried harder on that song. And sure enough, this time the Tree was taller than either boy. Terrific! We could hardly wait to get outside and sing some more with Mother. For now hope was a rapture of certainty.

To this day I cannot hear "O Little Town of Bethlehem," from however cracked a curbside organ, without hearing through and beyond it the clear, true voice of my mother. Nor hear that long-vanished sweetness without knowing that presently, somewhere, somehow a great door is going to open and disclose unearthly beauty. It is more than sixty years since our sitting-room door swung back for the fourth time, that night in the Old Colony of Massachusetts. But I can still see, sharp as life, the splendor of the Tree that towered to the ceiling in its glossy dark green, sparkling with silver tinsel, glowing with candles and half hiding in its crisp, fragrant needles, the incomparable perfection of spheres that shone like far-off other worlds, red and blue and green and gold . . .

Cynics say that miracles are all man-made—contrived, like a Christmas tree hidden in a closet and flashed upon wondering kids. That even the Christmas spirit is only a spell we work up to bemuse one

another—and then fall for, ourselves, like so many simple children. What of it? So much the better! If mankind, by its own devoted labor, can induce in itself—if only for a day—an all-pervading spirit of friendship and cheer and good will and loving kindness, that alone is a very great miracle. It is the kind of miracle that must please above all others Him who knows how miracles are wrought.

Robert Keith Leavitt

Heap on more wood!—the wind is chill;
But let it whistle as it will,
We'll keep our Christmas merry still.

Sir Walter Scott

Christmas with Mr. Pickwick

All three wended their way to the large kitchen, in which the family were by this time assembled, according to annual custom on Christmas eve, observed by old Wardle's forefathers from time immemorial.

From the centre of the ceiling of this kitchen old Wardle had just suspended with his own hands a huge branch of mistletoe, and this same branch of mistletoe instantaneously gave rise to a scene of general and most delightful struggling and confusion; in the midst of which Mr. Pickwick with a gallantry which would have done honour to a descendant of Lady Tollimglower herself, took the old lady by the hand, led her beneath the mystic branch, and saluted her in all courtesy and decorum. The old lady submitted to this piece of practical politeness with all the dignity which befitted so important and serious a solemnity,

but the younger ladies not being so thoroughly imbued with a supersti-
tious veneration of the custom, or imagining that the value of a salute is
very much enhanced if it cost a little trouble to obtain it, screamed and
struggled, and ran into corners, and threatened and remonstrated, and
did every thing but leave the room, until some of the less adventurous
gentlemen were on the point of desisting, when they all at once found it
useless to resist any longer, and submitted to be kissed with a good
grace. Mr. Winkle kissed the young lady with the black eyes, and Mr.
Snodgrass kissed Emily; and Mr. Weller, not being particular about the
form of being under the mistletoe, kissed Emma and the other female
servants, just as he caught them. As to the poor relations, they kissed
everybody, not even excepting the plainer portion of the young-lady
visitors, who, in their excessive confusion, ran right under the mistletoe, directly it was hung up, without knowing it! Wardle stood with his
back to the fire, surveying the whole scene, with the utmost satisfac-
tion; and the fat boy took the opportunity of appropriating to his own
use, and summarily devouring, a particularly fine mince pie, that had
been carefully put by, for somebody else.

Now the screaming had subsided, and faces were in a glow and curls

in a tangle, and Mr. Pickwick, after kissing the old lady as beforementioned, was standing under the mistletoe, looking with a very pleased countenance on all that was passing around him, when the young lady with the black eyes, after a little whispering with the other young ladies, made a sudden dart forward, and, putting her arm round Mr. Pickwick's neck, saluted him affectionately on the left cheek; and before Mr. Pickwick distinctly knew what was the matter, he was surrounded by the whole body, and kissed by every one of them.

It was a pleasant thing to see Mr. Pickwick in the centre of the group, now pulled this way, and then that, and first kissed on the chin and then on the nose, and then on the spectacles, and to hear the peals of laughter which were raised on every side; but it was a still more pleasant thing to see Mr. Pickwick, blinded shortly afterwards, with a silk-handkerchief, falling up against the wall, and scrambling into corners, and going through all the mysteries of blind-man's buff, with the utmost relish for the game, until at last he caught one of the poor relations; and then had to evade the blind-man himself, which he did with a nimbleness and agility that elicited the admiration and applause of all beholders. The poor relations caught just the people whom they

thought would like it; and when the game flagged, got caught themselves. When they were all tired of blind-man's buff, there was a great game at snap-dragon, and when fingers enough were burned with that, and all the raisins gone, they sat down by the huge fire of blazing logs to a substantial supper, and a mighty bowl of wassail, something smaller than an ordinary wash-house copper, in which the hot apples were hissing and bubbling with a rich look, and a jolly sound, that were perfectly irresistible.

"This," said Mr. Pickwick, looking round him, "this is, indeed, comfort."

Charles Dickens,
The Pickwick Papers

He is the happiest, be he king or
peasant, who finds peace in his home.

Goethe

It is more blessed to
give than to receive.

Acts 20:35 (KJV)

The Festival of Christmas

Of all the old festivals . . . that of Christmas awakens the strongest and most heartfelt associations. There is a tone of solemn and sacred feeling that blends with our conviviality, and lifts the spirit to a state of hallowed and elevated enjoyment. The services of the church about this season are extremely tender and inspiring; they dwell on the beautiful story of the origin of our faith, and the pastoral scenes that accompanied its announcement: they gradually increase in fervor and pathos during the season of Advent, until they break forth in full jubilee on the morning that brought peace and good-will to men. I do not know a grander effect of music on the moral feelings than to hear the full choir and the pealing organ performing a Christmas anthem in a cathedral, and filling every part of the vast pile with triumphant harmony.

It is a beautiful arrangement, also, derived from days of yore, that this

festival, which commemorates the announcement of the religion of peace and love, has been made the season for gathering together of family connections, and drawing closer again those bands of kindred hearts, which the cares and pleasures and sorrows of the world are continually operating to cast loose; of calling back the children of a family, who have launched forth in life, and wandered widely asunder, once more to assemble about the paternal hearth, that rallying-place of the affections, there to grow young and loving again among the endearing mementos of childhood. . . .

The pitchy gloom without makes the heart dilate on entering the room filled with the glow and warmth of the evening fire. The ruddy blaze diffuses an artificial summer and sunshine through the room, and lights up each countenance into a kindlier welcome. Where does the honest face of hospitality expand into a broader and more cordial smile—where is the shy glance of love more sweetly eloquent—than by the winter fireside? and as the hollow blast of wintry wind rushes through the hall, claps the distant door, whistles about the casement, and rumbles down the chimney, what can be more grateful than that feeling of sober and sheltering security, with which we look round upon the comfortable

chamber, and the scene of domestic hilarity?

The English, from the great prevalence of rural habits throughout every class of society, have always been fond of those festivals and holidays which agreeably interrupt the stillness of country life; and they were in former days particularly observant of the religious and social rites of Christmas. It is inspiring to read even the dry details which some antiquaries have given of the quaint humors, the burlesque pageants, the complete abandonment to mirth and good-fellowship, with which this festival was celebrated. It seemed to throw open every door, and unlock every heart. It brought the peasant and the peer together, and blended all ranks in one warm generous flow of joy and kindness. The old halls of castles and manor-houses resounded with the harp and the Christmas carol, and their ample boards groaned under the weight of hospitality. Even the poorest cottage welcomed the festive season with green decorations of bay and holly—the cheerful fire glanced its rays through the lattice, inviting the passenger to raise the latch, and join the gossip knot huddled round the hearth, beguiling the long evening with legendary jokes, and oft-told Christmas tales.

Washington Irving,
Old Christmas

It is a fine seasoning for joy to
think of those we love.

Molière

Scrooge's Nephew on Christmas

"There are many things from which I might have derived good, by which I have not profited, . . . Christmas among the rest. But I am sure I have always thought of Christmas time, when it has come round . . . as a good time; a kind, forgiving, charitable, pleasant time; the only time I know of, in the long calendar of the year, when men and women seem by one consent to open their shut-up hearts freely, and to think of people below them as if they really were fellow-passengers to the grave, and not another race of creatures bound on other journeys. And therefore, uncle, though it has never put a scrap of gold or silver in my pocket, I believe that it has done me good, and will do me good; and I say, God bless it!"

Charles Dickens,
A Christmas Carol

May joy come from God above
To all those who Christmas love.

13th Century Carol

The Gift of the Magi

One dollar and eighty-seven cents. That was all. And sixty cents of it was in pennies. Pennies saved one and two at a time by bulldozing the grocer and the vegetable man and the butcher until one's cheeks burned with the silent imputation of parsimony that such close dealing implied. Three times Della counted it. One dollar and eighty-seven cents. And the next day would be Christmas.

There was clearly nothing to do but flop down on the shabby little couch and howl. So Della did it. Which instigates the moral reflection that life is made up of sobs, sniffles, and smiles, with sniffles predominating.

While the mistress of the home is gradually subsiding from the first stage to the second, take a look at the home. A furnished flat at $8 per week. It did not exactly beggar description, but it certainly had that

word on the lookout for the mendicancy squad.

In the vestibule below was a letter-box into which no letter would go, and an electric button from which no mortal finger could coax a ring. Also appertaining thereunto was a card bearing the name "Mr. James Dillingham Young."

The "Dillingham" had been flung to the breeze during a former period of prosperity when its possessor was being paid $30 per week. Now, when the income was shrunk to $20, the letters of "Dillingham" looked blurred, as though they were thinking seriously of contracting to a modest and unassuming D. But whenever Mr. James Dillingham Young came home and reached his flat above he was called "Jim" and greatly hugged by Mrs. James Dillingham Young, already introduced to you as Della. Which is all very good.

Della finished her cry and attended to her cheeks with the powder rag. She stood by the window and looked out dully at a grey cat walking a grey fence in a grey backyard. Tomorrow would be Christmas Day, and she had only $1.87 with which to buy Jim a present. She had been saving every penny she could for months, with this result. Twenty dollars a week doesn't go far. Expenses had been greater than she had calculated.

They always are. Only $1.87 to buy a present for Jim. Her Jim. Many a happy hour she had spent planning for something nice for him. Something fine and rare and sterling—something just a little bit near to being worthy of the honor of being owned by Jim.

There was a pier-glass between the windows of the room. Perhaps you have seen a pier-glass in an $8 flat. A very thin and very agile person may, by observing his reflection in a rapid sequence of longitudinal strips, obtain a fairly accurate conception of his looks. Della, being slender, had mastered the art.

Suddenly she whirled from the window and stood before the glass. Her eyes were shining brilliantly, but her face had lost its color within twenty seconds. Rapidly she pulled down her hair and let it fall to its full length.

Now, there were two possessions of the James Dillingham Youngs in which they both took a mighty pride. One was Jim's gold watch that had been his father's and grandfather's. The other was Della's hair. Had the Queen of Sheba lived in the flat across the airshaft, Della would have let her hair hang out the window some day to dry just to depreciate Her Majesty's jewels and gifts. Had King Solomon been the janitor, with all

his treasures piled up in the basement, Jim would have pulled out his watch every time he passed, just to see him pluck at his beard from envy.

So now Della's beautiful hair fell about her, rippling and shining like a cascade of brown waters. It reached below her knee and made itself almost a garment for her. And then she did it up again nervously and quickly. Once she faltered for a minute and stood still while a tear or two splashed on the worn red carpet.

On went her old brown jacket; on went her old brown hat. With a whirl of skirts and with the brilliant sparkle still in her eyes, she fluttered out the door and down the stairs to the street. Where she stopped the sign read: "Mme. Sofronie. Hair Goods of All Kinds." One flight up Della ran, and collected herself, panting. Madame, large, too white, chilly, hardly looked the "Sofronie."

"Will you buy my hair?" asked Della.

"I buy hair," said Madame. "Take yer hat off and let's have a sight at the looks of it."

Down rippled the brown cascade.

"Twenty dollars," said Madame, lifting the mass with a practiced

hand.

"Give it to me quick," said Della.

Oh, and the next two hours tripped by on rosy wings. Forget the hashed metaphor. She was ransacking the stores for Jim's present.

She found it at last. It surely had been made for Jim and no one else. There was no other like it in any of the stores, and she had turned all of them inside out. It was a platinum fob chain simple and chaste in design, properly proclaiming its value by substance alone and not by meretricious ornamentation—as all good things should do. It was even worthy of The Watch. As soon as she saw it she knew that it must be Jim's. It was like him. Quietness and value—the description applied to both. Twenty-one dollars they took from her for it, and she hurried home with the 87 cents. With that chain on his watch Jim might be properly anxious about the time in any company. Grand as the watch was, he sometimes looked at it on the sly on account of the old leather strap that he used in place of a chain.

When Della reached home her intoxication gave way a little to prudence and reason. She got out her curling irons and lighted the gas and went to work repairing the ravages made by generosity added to love.

Which is always a tremendous task, dear friends—a mammoth task.

Within forty minutes her head was covered with tiny close-lying curls that made her look wonderfully like a truant schoolboy. She looked at her reflection in the mirror long, carefully, and critically.

"If Jim doesn't kill me," she said to herself, "before he takes a second look at me, he'll say I look like a Coney Island chorus girl. But what could I do—oh! what could I do with a dollar and eighty-seven cents?"

At 7 o'clock the coffee was made and the frying-pan was on the back of the stove hot and ready to cook the chops.

Jim was never late. Della doubled the fob chain in her hand and sat on the corner of the table near the door that he always entered. Then she heard his step on the stair away down on the first flight, and she turned white for just a moment. She had a habit of saying little silent prayers about the simplest everyday things, and now she whispered: "Please God, make him think I am still pretty."

The door opened and Jim stepped in and closed it. He looked thin and very serious. Poor fellow, he was only twenty-two—and to be burdened with a family! He needed a new overcoat and he was without gloves.

Jim stopped inside the door, as immovable as a setter at the scent of quail. His eyes were fixed upon Della, and there was an expression in them that she could not read, and it terrified her. It was not anger, nor surprise, nor disapproval, nor horror, nor any of the sentiments that she had been prepared for. He simply stared at her fixedly with that peculiar expression on his face.

Della wriggled off the table and went for him.

"Jim, darling," she cried, "don't look at me that way. I had my hair cut off and sold it because I couldn't have lived through Christmas without giving you a present. It'll grow out again—you won't mind, will you? I just had to do it. My hair grows awfully fast. Say 'Merry Christmas!' Jim, and let's be happy. You don't know what a nice—what a beautiful, nice gift I've got for you."

"You've cut off your hair?" asked Jim, laboriously, as if he had not arrived at that patent fact yet even after the hardest mental labor.

"Cut it off and sold it," said Della. "Don't you like me just as well, anyhow? I'm me without my hair, ain't I?"

Jim looked about the room curiously.

"You say your hair is gone?" he said, with an air almost of idiocy.

"You needn't look for it," said Della. "It's sold, I tell you—sold and gone, too. It's Christmas Eve, boy. Be good to me, for it went for you. Maybe the hairs of my head were numbered," she went on with a sudden serious sweetness, "but nobody could ever count my love for you. Shall I put the chops on, Jim?"

Out of his trance Jim seemed quickly to wake. He enfolded his Della. For ten seconds let us regard with discreet scrutiny some inconsequential object in the other direction. Eight dollars a week or a million a year—what is the difference? A mathematician or a wit would give you the wrong answer. The magi brought valuable gifts, but that was not among them. This dark assertion will be illuminated later on.

Jim drew a package from his overcoat pocket and threw it upon the table.

"Don't make any mistake, Dell," he said, "about me. I don't think there's anything in the way of a haircut or a shave or a shampoo that could make me like my girl any less. But if you'll unwrap that package you may see why you had me going a while at first."

White fingers and nimble tore at the string and paper. And then an ecstatic scream of joy; and then, alas! a quick feminine change to hys-

terical tears and wails, necessitating the immediate employment of all the comforting powers of the lord of the flat.

For there lay The Combs—the set of combs, side and back, that Della had worshipped for long in a Broadway window. Beautiful combs, pure tortoise shell, with jeweled rims—just the shade to wear in the beautiful vanished hair. They were expensive combs, she knew, and her heart had simply craved and yearned over them without the least hope of possession. And now, they were hers, but the tresses that should have adorned the coveted adornments were gone.

But she hugged them to her bosom, and at length she was able to look up with dim eyes and a smile and say: "My hair grows so fast, Jim!"

And then Della leaped up like a little singed cat and cried, "Oh, oh!"

Jim had not yet seen his beautiful present. She held it out to him eagerly upon her open palm. The dull precious metal seemed to flash with a reflection of her bright and ardent spirit.

"Isn't it a dandy, Jim? I hunted all over town to find it. You'll have to look at the time a hundred times a day now. Give me your watch. I want to see how it looks on it."

Instead of obeying, Jim tumbled down on the couch and put his

hands under the back of his head and smiled.

"Dell," said he, "let's put our Christmas presents away and keep 'em a while. They're too nice to use just at present. I sold the watch to get the money to buy your combs. And now suppose you put the chops on."

The magi, as you know, were wise men—wonderfully wise men who brought gifts to the Babe in the manger. They invented the art of giving Christmas presents. Being wise, their gifts were no doubt wise ones, possibly bearing the privilege of exchange in case of duplication. And here I have lamely related to you the uneventful chronicle of two foolish children in a flat who most unwisely sacrificed for each other the greatest treasures of their house. But in a last word to the wise of these days let it be said that of all who give gifts these two were the wisest. Of all who give and receive gifts, such as they are wisest. Everywhere they are wisest. They are the magi.

O. Henry

There Never Was Such a Goose!

Perhaps it was the pleasure the good Spirit had in showing off this power of his, or else it was his own kind, generous, hearty nature, and his sympathy with all poor men, that led him straight to Scrooge's clerk's; for there he went, and took Scrooge with him, holding to his robe; and on the threshold of the door the Spirit smiled, and stopped to bless Bob Cratchit's dwelling with the sprinklings of his torch. Think of that! Bob had but fifteen "Bob" a-week himself; he pocketed on Saturdays but fifteen copies of his Christian name and yet the Ghost of Christmas Present blessed his four-roomed house!

Then up rose Mrs. Cratchit, Cratchit's wife, dressed out but poorly in a twice-turned gown, but brave in ribbons, which are cheap and make a goodly show for sixpence; and she laid the cloth, assisted by Belinda Cratchit, second of her daughters, also brave in ribbons; while Master Peter Cratchit plunged a fork into the saucepan of potatoes, and getting

the corners of his monstrous shirt collar (Bob's private property, conferred upon his son and heir in honor of the day) into his mouth, rejoiced to find himself so gallantly attired, and yearned to show his linen in the fashionable Parks. And now two smaller Cratchits, boy and girl, came tearing in, screaming that outside the baker's they had smelt the goose, and known it for their own; and basking in luxurious thoughts of sage and onion, these young Cratchits danced about the table, and exalted Master Peter Cratchit to the skies, while he (not proud, although his collars nearly choked him) blew the fire, until the slow potatoes, bubbling up, knocked loudly at the saucepan-lid to be let out and peeled.

"What has ever got your precious father then?" said Mrs. Cratchit. "And your brother, Tiny Tim! And Martha warn't as late last Christmas Day by half an hour!"

"Here's Martha, mother," said a girl appearing as she spoke.

"Here's Martha, mother!" cried the two young Cratchits. "Hurrah! There's such a goose, Martha!"

"Why, bless your heart alive, my dear, how late you are!" said Mrs. Cratchit, kissing her a dozen times, and taking off her shawl and bon-

net for her with official zeal.

"We'd a deal of work to finish up last night," replied the girl, "and had to clear away this morning, mother!"

"Well! Never mind so long as you are come," said Mrs. Cratchit. "Sit ye down before the fire, my dear, and have a warm, Lord bless ye!"

"No, no! There's father coming," cried the two young Cratchits, who were everywhere at once. "Hide, Martha, hide!"

So Martha hid herself, and in came little Bob, the father, with at least three feet of comforter, exclusive of the fringe, hanging down before him; and his threadbare clothes darned up and brushed, to look seasonable; and Tiny Tim upon his shoulder. Alas for Tiny Tim, he bore a little crutch, and had his limbs supported by an iron frame!

"Why, where's our Martha?" cried Bob Cratchit, looking round.

"Not coming," said Mrs. Cratchit.

"Not coming!" said Bob, with a sudden declension in his high spirits; for he had been Tim's blood horse all the way from church, and had come home rampant. "Not coming upon Christmas Day!"

Martha didn't like to see him disappointed, if it were only in joke; so she came out prematurely from behind the closet door, and ran into his

arms, while the two young Cratchits hustled Tiny Tim, and bore him off into the wash-house, that he might hear the pudding singing in the copper.

"And how did little Tim behave?" asked Mrs. Cratchit, when she had rallied Bob on his credulity, and Bob had hugged his daughter to his heart's content.

"As good as gold," said Bob, "and better. Somehow he gets thoughtful, sitting by himself so much, and thinks the strangest things you ever heard. He told me, coming home, that he hoped the people saw him in the church, because he was a cripple, and it might be pleasant to them to remember, upon Christmas Day, who made lame beggars walk and blind men see."

Bob's voice was tremulous when he told them this, and trembled more when he said that Tiny Tim was growing strong and hearty.

His active little crutch was heard upon the floor, and back came Tiny Tim before another word was spoken, escorted by his brother and sister to his stool beside the fire; and while Bob, turning up his cuffs,—as if, poor fellow, they were capable of being made more shabby,—compounded some hot mixture in a jug with gin and lemons, and

stirred it round and round and put it on the hob to simmer, Master
Peter and the two ubiquitous young Cratchits went to fetch the goose,
with which they soon returned in high procession.

Such a bustle ensued that you might have thought a goose the rarest
of all birds; a feathered phenomenon, to which a black swan was a matter of course,—and in truth it was something very like it in that house.
Mrs. Cratchit made the gravy (ready beforehand in a little saucepan)
hissing hot; Master Peter mashed the potatoes with incredible vigor;
Miss Belinda sweetened up the applesauce; Martha dusted the hot
plates; Bob took Tiny Tim beside him in a tiny corner at the table; the
two young Cratchits set chairs for everybody, not forgetting themselves,
and mounting guard upon their posts, crammed spoons into their
mouths, lest they should shriek for goose before their turn came to be
helped.

At last the dishes were set on, and grace was said. It was succeeded
by a breathless pause, as Mrs. Cratchit, looking slowly all along the
carving-knife, prepared to plunge it in the breast; but when she did,
and when the long-expected gush of stuffing issued forth, one murmur
of delight arose all round the board, and even Tiny Tim, excited by the

two young Cratchits, beat on the table with the handle of his knife, and feebly cried Hurrah!

There never was such a goose. Bob said he didn't believe there ever was such a goose cooked. Its tenderness and flavor, size and cheapness, were the themes of universal admiration. Eked out by applesauce and mashed potatoes, it was a sufficient dinner for the whole family; indeed, as Mrs. Cratchit said with great delight (surveying one small atom of a bone upon the dish), they hadn't ate it all at last! Yet every one had had enough, and the youngest Cratchits in particular were steeped in sage and onion to the eyebrows! But now, the plates being changed by Miss Belinda, Mrs. Cratchit left the room alone—too nervous to bear witnesses—to take the pudding up, and bring it in.

Suppose it should not be done enough! Suppose it should break in turning out! Suppose somebody should have got over the wall of the back-yard, and stolen it, while they were merry with the goose,—a supposition at which the two young Cratchits became livid! All sorts of horrors were supposed.

Hallo! A great deal of steam! The pudding was out of the copper. A smell like a washing-day! That was the cloth. A smell like an eating-

house and a pastrycook's next door to each other, with a laundress's next door to that! That was the pudding! In half a minute Mrs. Cratchit entered—flushed, but smiling proudly—with the pudding, like a speckled cannon-ball, so hard and firm, blazing in half of half-a-quartern of ignited brandy, and bedight with Christmas holly stuck into the top.

O, a wonderful pudding! Bob Cratchit said, and calmly too, that he regarded it as the greatest success achieved by Mrs. Cratchit since their marriage. Mrs. Cratchit said that, now the weight was off her mind, she would confess she had had her doubts about the quantity of flour. Everybody had something to say about it, but nobody said or thought it was at all a small pudding for a large family. It would have been flat heresy to do so. Any Cratchit would have blushed to hint at such a thing.

At last the dinner was all done, the cloth was cleared, the hearth swept, and the fire made up. The compound in the jug being tasted, and considered perfect, apples and oranges were put upon the table, and a shovelful of chestnuts on the fire. Then all the Cratchit family drew round the hearth, in what Bob Cratchit called a circle, meaning half a

one; and at Bob Cratchit's elbow stood the family display of glass,—two tumblers, and a custard-cup without a handle.

These held the hot stuff from the jug, however, as well as golden goblets would have done; and Bob served it out with beaming looks; while the chestnuts on the fire sputtered and crackled noisily. Then Bob proposed:

"A merry Christmas to us all, my dears. God bless us!"

Which all the family re-echoed.

"God bless us every one!" said Tiny Tim, the last of all.

Charles Dickens,
A Christmas Carol

And numerous indeed are the hearts to which Christmas brings a brief season of happiness and enjoyment. How many families whose members have been dispersed and scattered far and wide, in the restless struggle of life, are then reunited, and meet once again in that happy state of companionship and mutual good-will, which is a source of such pure and unalloyed delight, and one so incompatible with the cares and sorrows of the world that the religious belief of the most civilized nations, and the rude traditions of the roughest savages, alike number it among the first days of a future state of existence, provided for the blest and happy! How many old recollections, and how many dormant sympathies, Christmas-time awakens!

We write these words now, many miles distant from the spot at which, year after year, we met in that day, a merry and joyous circle. Many of the hearts that throbbed so gaily then, have ceased to beat; . . . and yet the old house, the room, the merry voices and smiling faces, the jest, the laugh, the most minute and trivial circumstance connected

with those happy meetings, crowd upon our mind at each recurrence of the season, as if the last assemblage had been but yesterday. Happy, happy Christmas, that can win us back to the delusions of our childish days, recall to the old man the pleasures of his youth, and transport the traveler back to his own fireside and quiet home!

Charles Dickens

A Visit From St. Nicholas

'Twas the night before Christmas, when all through the house
Not a creature was stirring, not even a mouse;
The stockings were hung by the chimney with care,
In hopes that St. Nicholas soon would be there;
The children were nestled all snug in their beds,
While visions of sugar-plums danced through their heads;
And Mamma in her 'kerchief, and I in my cap,
Had just settled our brains for a long winter's nap,
When out on the lawn there arose such a clatter,
I sprang from my bed to see what was the matter.
Away to the window I flew like a flash,
Tore open the shutters and threw up the sash.
The moon on the breast of the new-fallen snow
Gave a lustre of mid-day to objects below,
When, what to my wondering eyes did appear,
But a miniature sleigh, and eight tiny reindeer,

With a little old driver so lively and quick,
I knew in a moment he must be St. Nick.
More rapid than eagles his coursers they came,
And he whistled, and shouted, and called them by name:
"Now, Dasher! now, Dancer! now, Prancer and Vixen!
On, Comet! on, Cupid! on, Donder and Blitzen!
To the top of the porch! to the top of the wall!
Now dash away! dash away! dash away, all!"
As leaves that before the wild hurricane fly,
When they meet with an obstacle, mount to the sky,
So up to the house-top the coursers they flew,
With the sleighful of toys, and St. Nicholas too—
And then in a twinkling, I heard on the roof
The prancing and pawing of each little hoof.
As I drew in my head, and was turning around,
Down the chimney St. Nicholas came with a bound.
He was dressed all in fur, from his head to his foot,
And his clothes were all tarnished with ashes and soot;
A bundle of toys he had flung on his back,
And he looked like a peddler just opening his pack.

His eyes—how they twinkled! his dimples, how merry!
His cheeks were like roses, his nose like a cherry!
His droll little mouth was drawn up like a bow,
And the beard on his chin was as white as the snow;
The stump of a pipe he held tight in his teeth,
And the smoke it encircled his head like a wreath;
He had a broad face and a round little belly
That shook when he laughed, like a bowl full of jelly.
He was chubby and plump, a right jolly old elf,
And I laughed when I saw him in spite of myself;
A wink of his eye and a twist of his head
Soon gave me to know I had nothing to dread;
He spoke not a word, but went straight to his work,
And filled all the stockings; then turned with a jerk,
And laying his finger aside of his nose,
And giving a nod, up the chimney he rose.
He sprang to his sleigh, to his team gave a whistle,
And away they all flew like the down of a thistle.
But I heard him exclaim ere he drove out of sight—
"Happy Christmas to all and to all a Good Night!"

Clement C. Moore

The Night After Christmas

Twas the night after Christmas, when all through the house
Every soul was abed, and as still as a mouse;
The stockings, so lately St. Nicholas's care,
Were emptied of all that was eatable there.
The Darlings had duly been tucked in their beds—
With very full stomachs, and pains in their heads.
I was dozing away in my new cotton cap,
And Nancy was rather far gone in a nap,
When out in the nurs'ry arose such a clatter,
I sprang from my sleep, crying—"What is the matter?"
I flew to each bedside—still half in a doze—
Tore open the curtains, and threw off the clothes;
While the light of the taper served clearly to show

The piteous plight of those objects below;
For what to the fond father's eyes should appear
But the little pale face of each sick little dear?
For each pet that had crammed itself full as a tick,
I knew in a moment now felt like Old Nick.
Their pulses were rapid, their breathings the same,
What their stomachs rejected I'll mention by name—
Now Turkey, now Stuffing, Plum Pudding, of course,
And Custards, and Crullers, and Cranberry sauce;
Before outraged nature, all went to the wall,
Yes—Lollypops, Flapdoodle, Dinner, and all;
Like pellets which urchins from popguns let fly,
Went figs, nuts and raisins, jam, jelly and pie,
Till each error of diet was brought to my view,
To the shame of Mamma and Santa Claus, too.
I turned from the sight, to my bedroom stepped back,
And brought out a phial marked "Pulv. Ipecac.,"
When my Nancy exclaimed—for their sufferings shocked her—
"Don't you think you had better, love, run for the Doctor?"
I ran and was scarcely back under my roof,

When I heard the sharp clatter of old Jalap's hoof.
I might say that I hardly had turned myself round,
When the Doctor came into the room with a bound.
He was covered with mud from his head to his foot,
And the suit he had on was his very worst suit;
He had hardly had time to put that on his back,
And he looked like a Falstaff half fuddled with sack.
His eyes, how they twinkled! Had the Doctor got merry?
His cheeks looked like Port and his breath smelled of Sherry.
He hadn't been shaved for a fortnight or so,
And the beard on his chin wasn't white as the snow.
But inspecting their tongues in despite of their teeth,
And drawing his watch from his waistcoat beneath,
He felt of each pulse, saying—"Each little belly
Must get rid"—here he laughed—"of the rest of that jelly."
I gazed on each chubby, plump, sick little elf,
And groaned when he said so, in spite of myself;
But a wink of his eye when he physicked our Fred
Soon gave me to know I had nothing to dread.
He didn't prescribe, but went straightway to work

And dosed all the rest, gave his trousers a jerk,
And, adding directions while blowing his nose,
He buttoned his coat; from his chair he arose,
Then jumped in his gig, gave old Jalap a whistle,
And Jalap dashed off as if pricked by a thistle;
But the Doctor exclaimed, ere he drove out of sight,
"They'll be well by tomorrow—good night, Jones, good night!"

Anonymous